ASK BETTER QUESTIONS

The One Skill That Improves Every Relationship and Meeting

Elias Grant

Asher Rohi Publishing

asherrohipublishing.com

Copyright

For everyone who has ever walked away from a conversation thinking, "I wish I had asked more."

Table of Contents

Introduction

The Question You Stopped Asking

It is a Tuesday evening and you are sitting across from someone you love.

Maybe it is dinner. Maybe the television is on in the background and neither of you is really watching it. Your partner, or your oldest friend, or your grown child who came home for the weekend is telling you something — about their day, their week, a problem they have been carrying — and you are nodding, and making the right sounds, and somewhere in the middle of their second sentence your mind has already begun composing your response.

You are not listening. Not really. You are waiting.

And when they finish, you say something — something kind, probably, something relevant — and the conversation moves on. And nobody notices. And nothing goes wrong. And later that evening, lying in the dark, you have the faint and uncomfortable sense that you were in the room but not quite present. That they spoke and you heard but did not receive. That something was available in that conversation that you did not reach for.

What you did not reach for was a question.

Not a polite question. Not "how was your day" or "did that get sorted?" — the questions that are really just sounds we make to signal that we are still paying attention. A real question. The kind that says: I want to know what is actually happening inside you. I am not in a hurry. I am interested in your answer more than I am interested in giving you mine.

That question would have cost you almost nothing. And it might have changed everything about that conversation.

* * *

Here is what that missed question cost you.

Not the conversation itself — conversations recover, evenings move on. What it cost you was information you will never now have. The thing behind the thing they were telling you. The worry underneath the anecdote, the longing inside the update, the version of that person that only emerges when someone asks the right question and then waits, , for the answer.

This is happening every day, in every direction, across every relationship and every meeting and every interaction that matters to you. You are moving through your life in close proximity to other people — colleagues, friends, the people you share a home with — and you are skimming the surface of them. Getting the summary. Missing the depth.

And it is not because you do not care. It is because nobody ever taught you to ask.

The cost shows up in your work — in the decisions made on assumptions that a single good question would have corrected, in the relationships with colleagues that never quite deepened into trust, in the meetings that ended without anyone having said the thing that actually needed saying.

It shows up in your personal life — in the friendships that thinned out slowly over years until all that was left was logistics, in the conversations with your parents or your children that stayed safely on the surface, in the moments with your partner when connection was available and you both somehow missed it.

And it shows up in your relationship with yourself — in the quality of the questions you ask about your own life, your own choices, your own possibilities. The internal questions most of us run on are not designed to open things up. They are designed to confirm what we already believe.

Learning to ask better questions will not fix all of this. But it will begin to.

*   *   *

There is a reason questions land differently than statements. It is not social. It is neurological.

When your brain hears a question — any question — it triggers an involuntary search process. Neuroscientists call it instinctive elaboration. You cannot hear a question without your brain beginning to hunt for an answer, even when you have no desire to engage, even when the question is unwelcome, even when you are trying not to think about it. A statement can be ignored. A question cannot. It gets inside. It sets something in motion that does not easily stop.

This is why questions change people in ways that arguments rarely do. You can deflect a statement. You can dismiss a piece of advice. But a question — a real one, aimed precisely — bypasses the defences and puts the other person's own brain to work on your behalf. The most effective leaders, the most trusted therapists, the most persuasive negotiators in the world are not the ones with the best arguments. They are the ones with the best questions.

Research at Harvard Business School found something that should stop most of us cold. People who ask more questions — and particularly those who ask follow-up questions, the ones that say I heard what you just said and I want to know more — are rated significantly more likeable, more intelligent, and more trustworthy by the people they speak with. Not slightly more. Significantly more.

But here is what the same research found about how the questioners feel: worse. Not better. People who ask more questions consistently report feeling that they contributed less to the conversation. That they appeared less competent. That they talked too little and gave too little of their expertise. The gap between how asking feels and what it actually produces is one of the most striking findings in the field of human communication.

You have been avoiding something that makes you look more capable because it makes you feel less capable. That is worth sitting with.

And then there is the question of where this gap came from. Research on child development tells us that children between the ages of two and five ask somewhere between one hundred and three hundred questions per day. They are relentlessly, exhaustingly, magnificently curious. They question everything — why the sky is that color, why that person looks sad, why we do things the way we do them. Questions are their primary tool for making sense of the world.

By the time those same children reach secondary school, the number has collapsed to almost zero.

What happened? Twelve years of education happened. Twelve years in rooms where questions were the tool of the teacher and answers were the expected output of the student. Twelve years of being graded, assessed, ranked, and rewarded for what you knew — and never once evaluated on the quality of what you asked. By the time most people enter adulthood they have been systematically, comprehensively, and entirely unintentionally trained out of one of the most powerful tools they were born with.

You did not lose your curiosity. It was taken from you, a little at a time, by a system that did not know what it was doing.

*   *   *

So let us be precise about what the problem actually is.

It is not that you are incurious. It is not that you are self-absorbed, or a bad listener, or someone who simply does not care enough about other people to ask about them. Those are the stories people tell themselves — and they are almost never true.

The real problem is that you were shaped by a culture that treats questions as a form of exposure. In most professional environments, certainty is currency. The person who knows is respected. The person who asks is suspected of not knowing. And so over years — in meetings, in classrooms, in performance reviews and presentations and first impressions — you learned to lead with what you know rather than what you are curious about.

That conditioning does not disappear when you walk out of the office, or close your laptop, or sit down to dinner with the people who matter most to you. It follows you everywhere. It is running quietly in the background of every conversation you have ever had.

The good news is that conditioning can be undone. Not instantly. Not without some discomfort. But deliberately, with the right tools, in a way that compounds over time.

The place to start is understanding what was actually taken from you — and why getting it back requires something that no one in your education ever asked you to develop.

Courage.

*   *   *

The best questioners in the world are not necessarily the most curious people in the room. They are the most courageous.

Think about what it actually takes to ask a genuine question — one you do not already know the answer to, one that does not have a polite or expected response baked into it, one that says: I do not have this figured out and I am more interested in your answer than I am in managing what you think of me.

In most social situations, that is a vulnerable position to occupy. Certainty performs confidence. Questions admit uncertainty. And uncertainty, in a culture that has spent decades rewarding the appearance of having it together, feels dangerous.

This is why so many people reach for statements when they should be asking. Statements feel like solid ground. Questions feel like stepping off the edge of something. And so we fill the silence with our own experience, our own opinions, our own well-meaning advice — not because we do not care about the other person's answer, but because asking for it feels, in some way we cannot quite name, like a risk.

What this book is teaching, underneath all the technique and the science and the practical tools, is the capacity to tolerate that open space. To become someone who can ask a question and then wait — actually wait, without filling the silence, without softening the question into a statement, without rushing to supply the answer yourself — for another person's genuine response.

That is not a communication skill. That is a form of courage. And like all forms of courage, it gets easier every time you practise it.

Here is what this book will do, and what it will not.

It will not give you a set of clever techniques to deploy on unsuspecting colleagues in your next meeting. It will not make you sound like a therapist. It will not turn you into the kind of person who asks follow-up questions while secretly waiting for their turn to talk — which is its own particular kind of performance, and one that most people can feel from across a room.

What it will give you is a clear understanding of why questions work the way they do — the neuroscience, the social science, and the practical mechanics — so that when the moment arrives and there is no script available, you still know what to do and why. A set of specific, practical tools for the situations where your questions most often fail you. And a framework for thinking about questions not as a technique you apply but as an orientation you develop — a genuine, sustained curiosity that produces the right question naturally, rather than requiring you to remember a formula.

This is a short book. Every chapter is built around one idea you can use today. The goal is not that you finish it feeling informed. It is that you put it down and immediately have a different conversation with someone — and that they feel it.

* * *

Think of the person you are closest to in the world.

It might be your partner, a parent, an old friend — someone who has known you long enough that the conversations between you have their own familiar grooves, their own comfortable rhythms, their own reliable routes around the things that are harder to say.

How many questions did you ask them today?

And of those questions — the real ones, if there were any — how many did you already know the answer to before you asked?

That gap, between the questions you asked and the ones you could have asked, between the surface of the conversation and the depth that was available just below it — that gap is what this book is about.

Let's go find out what is on the other side of it.

Chapter 1

Why Most People Ask Terrible Questions

Picture the most knowledgeable person you know.

Maybe it is your manager, the one who has been in the industry for twenty years and has seen every variation of every problem that walks through the door. Maybe it is a parent, or an older sibling, or a mentor who cares about you and wants to help. Maybe it is you — in the domain where you have accumulated the most experience, the place where you know more than almost anyone in the room.

Now picture that person in a conversation where someone is describing a problem.

The knowledgeable person listens for thirty seconds — maybe a minute, if they are being patient. And then, before the other person has quite finished, before the full shape of the problem has had a chance to emerge, the expert leans forward. They ask a question.

"Have you tried talking to HR about it?"

"Did you consider just reframing the whole project?"

"Wouldn't it be simpler to just start over from scratch?"

The person describing the problem pauses. Something shifts in the room — subtle, almost invisible, but there. They give a short answer. The conversation moves on. And somewhere in the person who was describing the problem, a small door closes. Not dramatically. Not with any resentment. Just quietly. They have learned, without being told, that this is not a conversation where the full version of the problem is welcome.

The expert, meanwhile, is completely unaware that anything went wrong. They asked a question, didn't they? They were engaged, curious, helpful. What is the problem?

The problem is that what they asked was not a question. It was an answer wearing a question mark. And the person on the receiving end felt it — even if neither of them could explain why.

This is not a story about bad people. It is a story about what questions are actually doing in most conversations — and why the gap between what we think they are doing and what they are actually doing is costing us more than we know.

* * *

Here is something that communication books almost never say: there is no such thing as a neutral question.

Every question you ask is doing a job. It is performing a function in the conversation — managing something, protecting something, confirming something, filling something. And in the vast majority of everyday exchanges, that job has very little to do with genuine curiosity about another person's inner experience.

Consider what your questions are actually hired to do.

Some questions are hired to protect status. When someone with expertise asks "Don't you think we should go with option A?" they are not curious about the answer. They have already decided. The question is advocacy in disguise — a way of advancing a position while maintaining the appearance of openness. Leading questions are the most common instrument of status protection in professional life, and they are so habitual that the people who use them most often are entirely unaware they are doing it.

Some questions are hired to confirm assumptions. We ask questions not to discover what someone thinks but to verify that they think what we already believe. "That was difficult for you, wasn't it?" is not curiosity. It is a presumption seeking validation. The question has an answer baked in, and any answer that deviates from it feels, to the questioner, like the other person got it wrong.

Some questions are hired to manage silence. The pause after someone has finished speaking feels, to most people, like something that needs to be fixed. And so we reach for a question — not because we want the answer, but because the silence is uncomfortable and a question is the most socially acceptable way to fill it.

Some questions are hired to perform interest. We have all been in conversations where we have asked a follow-up question not because we wanted the answer but because we wanted to appear engaged. The question is a social signal — I am listening, I am present, I care — that is sent without any genuine intention to receive what comes back.

And some questions are hired to steer. They appear open — "What do you think we should do here?" — but the acceptable range of answers is narrow. The question creates the impression of consultation while actually pointing toward a predetermined destination.

None of this is malicious. Every single one of these functions is entirely human and entirely understandable. But they are using the form of a question to accomplish something other than curiosity. And the person on the receiving end — their gut, whatever it is that registers the quality of attention being paid to them — feels the difference every single time.

* * *

The research on why this happens is both humbling and clarifying.

The first finding comes from the work of organisational psychologist Pamela Hinds at Stanford, who studied what happens to people as they develop expertise in a domain. What she found has a name — the curse of expertise — and it is more pervasive and more damaging than most people realize.

As you accumulate knowledge and experience in any area of your life, you become systematically less able to remember what it was like not to know. This means that the more experience you bring to a conversation, the less access you have to genuine curiosity about the other person's experience — because your experience keeps telling you that you already know what theirs is like. The expert who begins solving your problem before you finish describing it is not arrogant. They are neurologically compromised by their own competence. Their brain has so efficiently pattern-matched your situation to the ones they have seen before that genuine curiosity about what is different or particular about your version of it has been largely foreclosed.

The most dangerous conversational position is not ignorance. It is the false certainty that comes from knowing too much.

This connects directly to the second finding, from Nicholas Epley at the University of Chicago. Epley has spent years studying the gap between what we think we know about other people's inner experiences and what those experiences actually are. His findings are consistent and striking: people drastically overestimate how accurately they can predict what others think, feel, want, and intend. And the people who most overestimate their understanding of others are those who have spent the most time with them. Long-term partners. Close colleagues. Old friends.

Familiarity does not produce understanding. It produces the comfortable illusion of understanding. And the only antidote, Epley's research consistently shows, is direct inquiry. Asking. Not assuming you know — actually checking.

The third finding comes from Julia Minson at Harvard Kennedy School, and it explains why some questions feel like attacks even when they are clearly not intended as one. Her work demonstrates that questions with embedded assumptions trigger defensiveness as reliably and as powerfully as direct criticism. "Why did you make such a risky call?" and "You made a risky call, and I think you were wrong" produce almost identical emotional responses in the person being asked — even though one is technically a question.

Compare that to "What were you weighing up when you made that call?" The words are remarkably similar. The experience of being asked is entirely different. One opens a door. The other closes it and slides a note under it requesting a defence.

Most people have no idea that their questions are doing this. They ask with genuine curiosity and receive defensive responses — and they conclude that the other person is being difficult, rather than that the question itself was experienced as a challenge.

* * *

There is one more way most people destroy their own questions — and it happens after the question has been asked.

You ask something real. Something open, something that could go anywhere. The other person hears it. They pause.

And then you fix it.

You restate the question in different words. You add a clarification that was not needed. You offer them an answer to choose from. You do whatever is necessary to fill the silence that has opened up — because the silence feels like failure, and failure feels like something that needs to be corrected immediately.

The research on conversational silence is unambiguous: when someone pauses after being asked a genuine question, they are thinking. The pause is not confusion. It is cognition — the other person's brain working on the problem you have given it. The silence is not the question failing. It is the question working.

But for most people, ten seconds of silence after a question feels like an eternity. The urge to fill that space is not a rational decision. It is a reflex. And like all reflexes, it operates faster than conscious thought.

The consequence is that most people never discover what their questions were capable of producing. They rescue the other person from the productive discomfort of genuine reflection — the discomfort that, if tolerated for just a few more seconds, would have produced something neither party expected.

Think of any conversation you have had with a great listener. What you probably remember, even if you could not name it at the time, is that they let things breathe. They asked something and then they were simply — unhurriedly, unhelpfully, magnificently — quiet. And into that quiet you said things you had not planned to say. Things that surprised you. Things that needed saying.

That quiet was not passive. It was the most active thing happening in the room.

Ask the question. And then — for ten seconds longer than feels comfortable — do nothing.

* * *

A good question does something that no statement, however eloquent, can do. It creates access.

Not access to information — though information often follows. Access to thinking that was not previously available to the person being asked.

The right question at the right moment opens a door in someone's mind that they could not have opened alone. "What would you do if you knew the decision could not be undone?" does not just ask — it creates a new space for the other person to think inside.

A good question also signals something that cannot be faked: genuine regard. People register the quality of attention being paid to them with extraordinary accuracy. You can perform interest — nodding, making encouraging sounds, asking follow-up questions — and the person you are performing for will feel, at some level, that they are being processed rather than received. But a question that comes from real curiosity communicates something no statement can replicate. It says: you are more interesting to me than my own thoughts about you.

And finally, a good question reveals what you do not know. This sounds obvious. It is rarer than it sounds. Most conversations confirm what we already believe. A question — a real one, aimed at the edge of what you understand — is one of the few mechanisms by which you can discover that your model of reality is incomplete before that incompleteness costs you something you cannot recover.

* * *

Here is something you can do in your next conversation — not eventually, not after practising for a month, but the next time you are about to ask someone something that matters.

Before the question leaves your mouth, run three checks. Three seconds, three questions, asked silently to yourself.

First: Do I already know the answer I want? If you do, you are not asking a question. You are making an argument and dressing it in a question mark. Make it In practice,, as a statement. The person you are talking to deserves to know when you are trying to persuade them rather than seeking their view.

Second: Am I asking this to fill silence or to hear the answer? If the question is driven by discomfort with the pause rather than genuine curiosity about what is on the other side of it, wait. Let the silence breathe for three more seconds. Something more honest will usually arrive.

12

Third: Does this question contain an assumption about the answer? Scan the question for embedded presumptions — "Don't you think...", "Surely you would agree...", "Wasn't it obvious that..." All of these have the answer baked in. Strip the presumption out. What remains is the real question.

Three seconds. Three checks. This is not a formula to be applied mechanically in every exchange. It is a practice for conversations that matter.

And it will feel slow at first. A one-second pause before a question reads as thoughtfulness, not hesitation. And the question that emerges on the other side of that pause will be a better question than the one that was ready before you checked.

The Exercise

Today — or in your next meaningful conversation, whichever comes first — apply one rule only.

Ask every question twice in your head before you ask it once out loud.

The first version that arrives will almost always be one of the questions described in this chapter — closed, leading, assumption-laden, or driven by the urge to fill silence. Notice it. Do not judge it. Then ask yourself: what am I actually curious about here?

The second question is usually the real one.

For three conversations this week, write down both versions — the question that arrived first and the question you asked instead. The gap between them is the most honest map of your questioning habits you will ever have.

Chapter Summary

- Most questions are not failed attempts at curiosity — they are successful attempts at something else: protecting status, confirming assumptions, managing silence, performing interest, or steering toward a predetermined destination.

- Expertise is the enemy of curiosity. The most knowledgeable person in any conversation is statistically the most likely to stop asking — and the most likely to be wrong about what the other person is actually experiencing.

- Familiarity produces the illusion of understanding. The people you know best are the people you are most likely to have stopped asking about. Only direct inquiry closes the gap.

- A good question creates access to new thinking, signals genuine regard, and reveals what you do not yet know. These are not small things. They are the building blocks of every relationship, team, and decision that has ever worked.

- The three-second audit — do I know the answer I want, am I asking to fill silence, does this embed an assumption — is the single most effective tool for catching a bad question before it leaves your mouth.

Chapter 2

The Anatomy of a Great Question

Picture two interviewers. Same role to fill. Same candidate sitting across from them.

The first interviewer leans forward, curious, and asks: "Tell me about a challenge you've faced at work."

The candidate smiles. They have rehearsed this. "Sure — we had a major project deadline that was at risk, and I had to rally the team to pull it back. We made it with two days to spare." The interviewer nods. They write something down. The conversation moves on.

The second interviewer leans forward — equally genuine — and asks: "What's the hardest decision you've ever had to walk away from without knowing if it was right?"

The candidate pauses. A real pause, not a performance one. Something shifts in their expression. And then they say something the interviewer was not expecting — something honest, something specific, something that reveals more about who this person actually is than anything in the carefully prepared resume in front of them.

Both interviewers asked open questions. Both were curious. But one of them asked a question that went somewhere. And the difference between those two questions is not technique. It is architecture.

* * *

The most common advice about questioning is to ask open questions rather than closed ones. This advice is not wrong. But it is incomplete in a way that matters.

Research by Karen Huang at Harvard found that the relationship between question type and conversation quality is far more nuanced than the open/closed distinction suggests. An open question asked without genuine curiosity produces worse outcomes than a closed question asked with it. The mechanism matters more than the form. Which means that teaching someone to ask open questions without teaching them what makes a question work at a deeper level is like teaching someone to smile without explaining what warmth is.

The person who has been told to "ask more open questions" and still finds that their conversations do not deepen — that the other person gives perfectly polite but perfectly surface answers — is not failing at technique. They are missing something structural. And structure is learnable.

* * *

Every great question shares four qualities. Not types — qualities. The distinction matters because qualities are architectural: they can be present in any question, regardless of how it is phrased. A closed question can have all four. An open question can have none.

The first quality is specificity. A specific question signals that you have been paying attention. It narrows the question to a size the respondent can actually engage with, rather than a scope so broad it produces a generic answer.

"What has been the most difficult part of this week?" produces a richer response than "How have you been?" — not because it is more open, but because it is more precise. The specificity communicates something the broader question cannot: I have noticed something about you and I am asking about that, not about you in general. People respond differently to questions that feel personal than to questions that feel formulaic. Specificity is what makes the difference.

The second quality is genuine curiosity. Not performed. Not tactical. The real thing. A question asked from genuine curiosity has a different quality from one asked from social obligation — and people register the difference at a level below conscious thought. Genuine curiosity cannot be faked for long, but it can be cultivated. The prerequisite is surrendering the need to already have the answer. This is where the courage framing from the introduction pays off: genuine curiosity requires the willingness to not know. And for most people, not knowing has been so thoroughly penalised that the willingness to inhabit it has to be consciously rebuilt.

The third quality is non-embedded judgment. Non-judgment in a question is not a matter of tone. It is structural. A question that contains no implied correct answer creates a space where the respondent can say anything without feeling measured against a standard they cannot see.

The test is simple: is there an answer to this question that would feel wrong to give? If yes, the question is not non-judgmental — regardless of how warm the questioner's expression is, regardless of how soft their voice. The evaluation is in the architecture. "Why did you do it that way?" has a wrong answer built in. "What were you going for when you made that call?" does not. Rewriting the first question as the second is not a matter of softening a delivery. It is a matter of structural revision.

The fourth quality is possibility orientation. The most generative questions do not root the respondent in the current problem. They ask the person to step slightly outside their present constraints and describe something they have not yet fully articulated — a preferred future, an unexplored option, an imagined solution.

"What would it look like if this went better than you expect?" produces access to thinking that "What's wrong right now?" cannot reach. The architecture of the question determines the architecture of the thinking it produces. Questions rooted in problems produce problem-thinking. Questions rooted in possibility produce possibility-thinking. This is not optimism for its own sake. It is a practical tool for expanding the range of what a conversation can produce.

* * *

Of all the insights in the research on questioning, the one most worth slowing down for is this: follow-up questions are the single highest-leverage question type available to you.

The Harvard research that established the likeability effect of questioning found something more specific when it looked closer. Follow-up questions — the ones that emerge directly from what someone just said — produced stronger positive effects on perceived likeability, trust, and conversation quality than any other question type. Not because they are grammatically superior. Because they cannot be faked.

You can prepare an opening question. You cannot prepare a follow-up. A follow-up requires that you were actually listening to the answer — that you absorbed what was said, noticed something specific in it, and chose to go deeper into that specific thing rather than moving to your next prepared point. A follow-up is proof of presence. It tells the other person, more clearly than any statement can, that their words arrived.

Three types of follow-up are worth keeping in your repertoire, not as scripts but as instincts to develop.

The deepening follow-up takes one word or phrase from the answer and asks about it directly. If someone says "it was more complicated than I expected," the deepening follow-up is simply: "What made it complicated?" That one question often yields more genuine information than the entire conversation that preceded it.

The feeling follow-up moves from the content of what was said to the experience of it. "What was that like for you?" is the simplest version. Most people — especially in professional contexts — ask about events and decisions but rarely ask about the human experience of those things. When you do, people open up in ways that surprise even them.

The implication follow-up asks about the consequence or meaning of what was shared, not the thing itself. "What does that change for you going forward?" moves the conversation from reporting to reflecting — which is where insight lives.

* * *

Neil Rackham's research on expert negotiators identified a pattern consistent enough to be striking: experts asked about implications and needs while average performers asked about facts and positions. The surface question is what you ask. The question behind it is what you actually want to know.

A doctor who asks "Where does it hurt?" wants to know the location of the pain. But the question behind that question — the one the skilled clinician is always working toward — is: what is actually wrong with you? The surface question is a route. The deeper question is the destination.

In everyday conversation, most people ask the surface question and stop there. The expert questioner gets the surface answer and immediately asks: what deeper question does this open up? What does this tell me that I need to know more about? And then they ask that.

Every follow-up, at its best, is the surface answer pointing the questioner toward the question beneath it.

* * *

There is one more tool worth naming, and it is counterintuitive enough to be worth emphasis.

"Tell me more." Two words. No question mark. No grammatical interrogative. And yet the research on active listening and therapeutic communication consistently shows that this construction — and its functional relatives, "say more about that," "keep going" — produces richer, more honest, and more generative responses than most carefully constructed open questions.

Why? Because it contains zero evaluative structure. There is no implied correct direction. There is no scope limitation. There is no framing that might accidentally signal what the right answer looks like. The other person can go anywhere — and that complete freedom is what produces the most honest answer.

A question is not a grammatical form. It is an act of genuine curiosity that creates space for another person's thinking. Sometimes that act wears a question mark. Often the most powerful version does not need one.

The practical takeaway: before reaching for a prepared question, consider whether "tell me more" would serve better. In most conversations about something that matters, it will.

The Exercise

Take a conversation you have coming up — a meeting, a difficult exchange, a catch-up with someone you have not spoken to properly in a while.

Write three questions you might ask in that conversation. Then run each one through the four-quality check: Is it specific enough to feel personal? Does it come from genuine curiosity? Does it embed a judgment? Does it open a door or close one?

For every question that fails a check, rewrite it until it passes. The rewritten version will almost always be shorter, more direct, and more open than the original. It will also feel slightly more exposing to ask — which is the reliable signal that it is a better question.

Then, in the actual conversation, notice what the rewritten questions produce compared to your usual approach.

Chapter Summary

- The open/closed distinction is real but insufficient. An open question without genuine curiosity produces worse results than a closed question with it. The mechanism matters more than the form.

- Every great question shares four structural qualities: specificity that feels personal, genuine curiosity, non-embedded judgment, and a possibility orientation that opens rather than closes the thinking available to the respondent.

- Follow-up questions are the single highest-leverage question type — not because they are grammatically superior but because they cannot be faked. A follow-up is proof of presence.

- Every question has a question behind it. Expert questioners identify the deeper question first and find the most direct route to it, rather than stopping at the surface answer.

- "Tell me more" outperforms most questions because it contains zero evaluative structure. A question is an act of genuine curiosity — it does not always need a question mark.

Chapter 3

Questions That Build Trust

Think of the person you trust most in your life.

The person who, when you are in real trouble, is the first one you call. Not because they always have the right answer. Not because they will solve the problem. Because when you talk to them, you feel — , completely — heard. The problem does not necessarily get smaller when you speak to them. But you do.

Now think about what that person actually does in conversation.

Chances are they do not talk more than you. They do not offer unsolicited advice. They do not redirect your experience back toward themselves. They do not finish your sentences. What they do, almost certainly, is ask better follow-up questions than anyone else in your life. They say things like: "And then what happened?" and "What was that like?" and "What are you most worried about?" And they wait — , without impatience — for your answer.

You trust this person, at least in part, because they make you feel seen. And they make you feel seen because they ask in a way that communicates: your inner experience is the most interesting thing in this conversation.

This is not a coincidence. It is a mechanism. And it is one you can build into your own relationships.

* * *

Most people believe trust is built through disclosure — through the things you share about yourself. The more you reveal, the more trust you earn.

The research tells a more complicated story. Disclosure matters, but it is not primary. What matters most in the formation and deepening of trust is the experience of being received — the felt sense that what you share lands somewhere, that it is heard and valued and met with genuine interest rather than polite acknowledgment.

And the primary mechanism for that experience is being asked the right question at the right moment, by someone who actually waits for the answer.

Research by Alison Wood Brooks and her colleagues at Harvard shows that people who are asked more follow-up questions feel significantly better understood after a conversation — not just more liked by the person who asked, but more understood by them. The feeling of being understood is, it turns out, closely tied to the experience of being questioned well. When someone asks us something good and then receives our answer fully, something shifts. We feel known. And feeling known is the substrate from which trust grows.

The problem is that most people spend their conversational energy trying to be interesting rather than interested. They share, they impress, they demonstrate, they perform. What the research consistently shows is that these strategies are exactly backwards. The way to be found compelling by another person is not to show them how compelling you are. It is to treat them as if they are.

* * *

Three specific moves build trust through questioning, and each one does different work.

The first is the follow-up. This is the move described in the previous chapter — taking something specific from someone's answer and asking about it directly. But its trust-building function is worth making explicit. A follow-up does not just gather more information. It sends a signal that cannot be faked: I was actually here. I heard what you said. You matter enough that I want to go deeper.

Every conversation contains dozens of moments where a follow-up would be the most powerful available move, and most people miss all of them — not because they do not care, but because they are composing their next contribution rather than receiving the current one. Learning to follow up consistently is less a skill than a reorientation. It requires deciding that your job in a conversation is not to be impressive. It is to be present.

The second move is the reflect-back. This is simpler than it sounds. You take a word or phrase the other person used — not a summary of what they said, not your interpretation, but their actual words — and you repeat it back to them as an opening for more.

"More complicated than you expected?" said as a question is one of the most effective conversational moves available. It is simple to the point of feeling almost too simple. But its power comes precisely from its simplicity: it shows you heard the specific thing they said, it hands control of direction back to them entirely, and it creates zero pressure. There is no implied right answer. There is no evaluation. There is just: I noticed what you said, and I want more of it.

Most people never do this because it feels insufficient. It does not feel like a contribution. That feeling is wrong. The reflect-back is a contribution — a signal of full attention that most people receive far less often than they need.

The third move is the permission question. This is the question you ask before asking the harder question. "Can I ask you something about that?" or "Is this a good moment to get into it?" or "Would it be useful to think out loud about this together?"

The permission question is the most underused trust-building tool in most people's conversational repertoire. Its power is this: it communicates that you respect the other person's emotional state enough to check before entering it. It treats their experience as territory that belongs to them, not a resource that is available to you because you are curious. And it almost always gets a yes — because the act of being asked is itself so rare and so welcome that most people respond to it with an immediate opening.

* * *

There is a distinction the research supports but that most people navigate by feel: the difference between interrogation and inquiry.

Both involve questions. Both are attempts to know more about another person. But they feel entirely different to the person being asked — and the difference is not primarily about the questions themselves. It is about what the questioner does with the answers.

Interrogation uses answers as building blocks for the questioner's next point. Each answer is a step in a ladder the questioner has already built in their head. They ask, they receive, they fit the answer into a frame they brought with them, and they move to the next question. The person being interrogated feels used, even when the questions are well-intentioned. They sense that they are providing material for someone else's understanding rather than being understood themselves.

Inquiry does something different. It allows the answer to change the direction. It follows what the other person says rather than following a predetermined path. It is willing to be surprised. When an answer opens up something unexpected — a new concern, an unexplored dimension, a feeling that was not on the agenda — inquiry follows that. The person being inquired into feels the difference immediately. They feel led, rather than led through.

The practical distinction: interrogation comes to a conversation with questions ready. Inquiry comes to a conversation with questions ready — and is willing to abandon every single one of them if something more important emerges.

* * *

Trust does not build in a single conversation. It builds through a pattern of conversations over time — each one adding a small amount to a ledger the other person is keeping without knowing they are keeping it.

Every time you ask a good follow-up, a little trust is deposited. Every time you use the reflect-back, a little more. Every time you ask a permission question before going somewhere hard, the account grows. And every time you cut someone off, or redirect to yourself, or ask a leading question that puts them on the defensive, something is withdrawn.

Most people do not know what their trust balance looks like with the people around them. They do not know whether the people they care about feel known by them or politely tolerated. The only way to find out is to start asking — and to pay attention to what the quality of the answers tells you about whether people feel safe enough in your presence to give you the real version.

The Exercise

In your next meaningful conversation with someone you care about —
a friend, a family member, a colleague — apply one move only.

When they say something, resist the instinct to respond. Instead, take
one word or phrase from what they just said and reflect it back as a
question. Just that. One reflect-back, followed by actual silence.

Notice what comes after. Notice whether the conversation goes
somewhere it would not have gone if you had done what you were going
to do. Notice what you learn.

Chapter Summary

- Trust is built not through what you reveal but through what you
  ask — and through the quality of attention you bring to the
  answer.

- People feel trusted and understood primarily when they are
  asked good follow-up questions and feel received. The most
  effective trust-building move you can make is to be more
  interested than interesting.

- Three specific moves build trust through questioning: the
  follow-up (proof of presence), the reflect-back (proof of
  hearing), and the permission question (proof of respect for the
  other person's emotional state).

- The difference between interrogation and inquiry is not the
  questions. It is whether the answers are allowed to change the
  direction of the conversation.

- Trust is a ledger. Every good question makes a deposit. Knowing
  this changes how you approach every conversation with
  someone who matters to you.

Chapter 4

Questions at Work

Someone in a meeting asks: "What would need to be true for this plan to fail?"

The room goes quiet for a second — not an uncomfortable quiet, but the kind that happens when an unexpected question opens up space in a conversation that was already closing. And then, one by one, people begin to name things. A dependency that had been assumed but never verified. A market assumption that nobody had tested. A resource constraint that everyone had privately worried about but nobody had voiced.

Three minutes of conversation surfaces what two hours of planning had missed.

That is the value of a well-placed question at work. It is not just information-gathering. It is direction-changing. The most valuable person in many professional settings is not the one with the best answer. It is the one who asks the question nobody else thought to ask — and changes the outcome of the meeting before it ends.

* * *

The workplace is where most people's questions go most wrong, and where better questions would yield the highest return. Professional culture rewards certainty and penalises apparent ignorance. So people default to leading questions that confirm existing positions, closed questions that allow meetings to feel productive without producing anything, and silence in moments when genuine inquiry would have changed everything.

The result is a consistent set of failures that most organisations attribute to the wrong causes. Strategies fail because nobody asked whether the assumptions behind them were sound. Projects go over time and budget because nobody asked what could go wrong. Feedback conversations produce defensiveness rather than growth because they open with criticism rather than curiosity. Talented people leave without anyone understanding why, because nobody asked the right question while there was still time to act on the answer.

None of this is inevitable. And none of it requires structural change. It requires one person in the room willing to ask differently.

* * *

Research on group decision-making consistently shows that the most dangerous moment in any meeting is when consensus appears to have been reached too easily. The human tendency in groups is toward alignment — we suppress doubts, we round off concerns, we signal agreement faster than we actually feel it, because disagreement is socially costly. The result is a phenomenon called groupthink, in which intelligent people collectively commit to decisions that any one of them would have challenged if asked in private.

The antidote to groupthink is not a change in culture, a restructured meeting agenda, or a new facilitation methodology. The antidote is one question, asked sincerely, before the decision is confirmed.

"What are we assuming that might not be true?"

This question does several things simultaneously. It surfaces the hidden premises behind a plan — the things that have been accepted as given rather than examined. It creates permission for people to voice the doubts they have been suppressing. And it models the intellectual humility that high-performing teams consistently demonstrate: the willingness to challenge even the decisions you advocated for, because you care more about getting it right than about being right.

A related question, developed from research on pre-mortem analysis, does similar work from a different direction: "Imagine it is a year from now and this plan has failed. What went wrong?" By asking people to inhabit a hypothetical future failure, this question produces a different kind of thinking than asking about current risks — more specific, more honest, more useful. People who would hesitate to express a concern in the present tense will name it freely when it is framed as having already happened.

* * *

Feedback conversations are among the most important and most consistently mishandled exchanges in professional life. They fail from both directions — the person giving feedback opens with criticism and triggers defensiveness, and the person receiving feedback asks clarifying questions that the giver experiences as argument rather than inquiry.

Both failures have a question-based solution.

If you are giving feedback, the most effective first move is almost never a statement. It is a question. "How do you feel it went?" asked before you offer any evaluation does two things: it tells you whether the person's self-assessment is accurate (which determines how much work the feedback needs to do) and it activates the person's own diagnostic intelligence rather than immediately putting them in a defensive position. People who identify a problem themselves are incomparably more committed to solving it than people who have a problem named for them.

The question that most accelerates professional development — and that most people are too afraid to ask — is: "What is one thing I do that makes your job harder?" This is a question that requires genuine willingness to hear an uncomfortable answer. Most people avoid it for exactly that reason. But the people who ask it consistently, and receive the answer without deflecting, develop faster and earn more trust than those who wait for feedback to arrive at formally scheduled intervals.

If you are receiving feedback, the question that converts vague criticism into actionable information is: "Can you give me a specific example?" Vague feedback produces vague improvement. A specific example gives you something concrete enough to examine, understand, and change. Asking for it is not defensiveness. It is rigour. And most good managers will respect you more for it.

* * *

There is a question that high-performing professionals ask at the start of every new relationship — whether with a manager, a client, a new colleague, or a team — and it is one of the most powerful available in professional life.

"What does success look like from your perspective?"

This question does something no job description or project brief can. It tells you what the person in front of you actually cares about — what they will use to evaluate your work, what they will notice when it is missing, what they are hoping for that they may not have explicitly said. When you understand what someone's definition of success is, you can align your work to it in ways that make you indispensable rather than merely competent.

The question also changes the relationship. It signals that you are not just executing a task. You are a partner in an outcome. That signal tends to unlock a different quality of information — more candid, more complete — than the information people share with those they experience as contractors rather than collaborators.

Ask it at the start. Ask it again in the middle. Ask it any time you sense that what you are delivering and what they are hoping for have started to drift apart.

The Exercise

Before your next significant meeting, write down one question that nobody else in the room is likely to ask — a question that challenges an assumption, surfaces a risk, or opens a line of inquiry that the agenda has not made space for. Write it down before the meeting so you actually ask it.

After the meeting, note whether asking it changed the direction of the conversation, and what would have been missed if the question had not been asked.

Chapter Summary

- The most valuable person in most professional settings is not the one with the best answer. It is the one who asks the question nobody else thought to ask — and changes the outcome before it is too late.

- "What are we assuming that might not be true?" is among the most powerful questions available in professional life. It surfaces hidden premises, creates permission for dissent, and models the intellectual humility that distinguishes good teams from great ones.

- In feedback conversations, the first move should almost always be a question: "How do you feel it went?" activates the other person's own diagnostic intelligence rather than immediately triggering defensiveness.

- "Can you give me a specific example?" converts vague criticism into actionable information. It is not defensiveness. It is rigour.

- "What does success look like from your perspective?" is the question that transforms professional relationships from transactional to collaborative. Ask it at the start of every new working relationship.

Chapter 5

Questions at Home

"How was your day?"

The question that ends ten thousand conversations before they start. Not because the people asking it do not care. Because they do — and they have just used the one question that virtually guarantees they will not find out.

The person being asked knows what is expected. A brief answer. A summary. "Fine." "Busy." "Okay, I guess." The question signals its own answer: something general, something manageable, something that takes about fifteen seconds and does not require either party to go anywhere they have not already been.

This is not the fault of the question-asker. It is the fault of the question. And the remarkable thing is that almost everyone uses it — every day, with the people they love most, as if it were the best available option.

It is not. Not even close.

* * *

There is a particular cruelty to the fact that we ask worse questions of the people we love most than of almost anyone else in our lives. We prepare for job interviews. We think carefully about what to say to new acquaintances. We research before networking events. But with our partners, our children, our oldest friends — we improvise. We assume we already know the answers. We substitute familiarity for curiosity and call it intimacy.

Nicholas Epley's research on social projection shows exactly what happens when we do. The more time we spend with someone, the more confident we become in our model of them — and the less frequently we update that model with new information. Long-term partners consistently overestimate how well they understand each other's current feelings, desires, and concerns. Close friends do the same. The people we know best are the people we are most likely to have stopped actually asking.

What familiarity produces is not understanding. It is a map of the person we met — updated less and less frequently as the relationship deepens. And it is possible to spend years living with someone whose map in your head has not kept pace with who they have become.

The only way to close that gap is to ask. Not once, not as a grand gesture, but as a sustained practice — the daily choice to treat the person across from you as someone whose inner experience you have not yet fully understood, and may never fully understand, and that this is what makes them endlessly worth asking about.

* * *

The most common failure in partner conversations is not lack of care. It is lack of specificity. Dead-end questions produce dead-end answers.

A small set of question swaps, applied consistently, changes the quality of what is possible.

"How was your day?" invites a summary. "What was the best thing that happened today that I might not know about?" invites a story. The second question signals — in its specificity, in its acknowledgment that there is a whole life happening that you are not automatically privy to — that you want the real version, not the condensed one.

"Are you okay?" invites a yes or no. "What's on your mind?" invites what is actually there. The closed question gives the person an exit. The open question hands them a pen and says: write whatever is true.

"What do you need from me right now — advice, or just someone to listen?" is perhaps the single most conflict-preventing question available in a close relationship. People in distress almost always know which of these they need. They are almost never asked. And the cost of providing the wrong one — offering solutions when someone needed only to be heard, or sitting silently when someone needed direction — is a conversation that leaves both people feeling worse than when it started.

* * *

Children are natural questioners. Between the ages of two and five, a child's curiosity is essentially unlimited — they ask about everything, they accept no answer as final, and they treat the world as a permanent object of wonder. And then, somewhere around adolescence, most of them stop asking. Not because they stop being curious. Because they have been taught, through years of small corrections, that asking too many questions is inconvenient.

The best thing a parent can do, conversationally, is reverse this dynamic. Ask your children questions you do not know the answers to. Let them be the expert sometimes. Ask for their opinion on things before you have already formed yours. And when they share something — an experience, a worry, a moment of excitement — follow up rather than pivoting to advice.

"What was the hardest part of your day?" produces ten times more than "How was school?" — because it is specific, because it acknowledges that days have texture, and because it gives the child permission to name something difficult rather than just reporting the summary.

"What do you think would be fair in this situation?" is not just a parenting technique. It is a statement of respect. It says: your judgment matters here. I am not managing you. I am thinking alongside you.

"What are you proudest of that nobody noticed?" is a question children almost never get asked, and the answers are often remarkable. They do things every day that go completely unacknowledged. The question finds those things — and in finding them, tells the child something that no generic praise ever could: you are seen more specifically than you realized.

* * *

Friendships drift when the questions stop. The logistics of staying in contact continue — the birthday messages, the occasional catch-up, the group chats — but the depth that made the friendship worth having gradually disappears, until one day you realize that you have not had a real conversation in months.

The fix is simpler than a rebuilt friendship routine or a formal reconnection exercise. It is a single different question, asked in the next conversation.

"What have you changed your mind about recently?" reveals more about a person than any number of factual updates. It tells you how they are growing, what they are questioning, where their thinking has moved. People who are willing to answer this question — to identify a belief they have revised — are the people worth keeping close.

"What do you wish people asked you more about?" is the meta-question. It hands the other person the keys to the conversation and says: show me where you want to go. The answers are almost always surprising, and almost always open up something that would have stayed hidden if you had defaulted to the standard questions.

The Exercise

Tonight, ask one person at home a question you have never asked them before. Write it down before the conversation so you actually ask it, rather than meaning to and then not quite getting there.

The question should be specific enough that they cannot answer it with a single word, open enough that they could take it anywhere, and genuine enough that you actually want to hear the answer.

Chapter Summary

- Familiarity is the enemy of curiosity. The people you know best are the people whose inner experience you are most likely to have stopped asking about — and whose map inside your head has fallen furthest behind who they have become.

- Dead-end questions produce dead-end answers. "How was your day?" produces a summary. "What was the best thing that happened today that I might not know about?" produces a story. Specificity signals that you want the real version.

- "What do you need from me right now — advice, or just someone to listen?" is one of the most conflict-preventing questions available in a close relationship. People almost always know the answer. They are almost never asked.

- Asking children questions you do not know the answers to — and treating their answers with genuine interest — reverses the conversational pattern that trains curiosity out of them.

- Friendships drift when the questions stop. One different question, asked in the next conversation, can open what years of logistics have kept closed.

Chapter 6

Questions You Ask Yourself

"Why does this always happen to me?"

The moment you ask it, your brain gets to work. It searches — diligently, helpfully, efficiently — for evidence that bad things happen specifically to you. And it finds it, because the brain is extraordinarily good at finding evidence for whatever premise a question contains. You asked why bad things always happen to you. Your brain provides the case notes.

Now ask a different question. "What could I do about this?" Same situation. Different question. And your brain gets to work again — searching now not for evidence of victimhood but for options, possibilities, paths through. It finds those too. Because that is also what brains do. They answer the question they are given.

The quality of your life is, in no small part, determined by the quality of the questions you run on internally. Not the questions you ask other people. The questions you ask yourself, silently, automatically, hundreds of times a day — and that your brain answers with complete, unquestioning obedience.

* * *

Most people have no idea what their internal questions actually are. They experience them as thoughts, as feelings, as the ambient texture of their inner life — not as a set of questions they are continuously asking and their brain is continuously answering.

Research in cognitive behavioural therapy consistently identifies the most common destructive thought patterns as question-shaped. "Why am I like this?" generates self-criticism rather than insight — it is designed not to produce an answer but to punish. "What's wrong with me?" presupposes the answer: something is. "Why can't I ever get this right?" closes off possibility rather than opening it, because the word "ever" frames the failure as fixed and universal rather than specific and revisable.

These are not idle thoughts. They are active questions that your brain is continuously, diligently answering. And the answers are making you worse at your life — not because you are weak, but because the questions were designed to produce those answers. They were not selected for their usefulness. They were absorbed, over years, from the environments that shaped you — from parents, from schools, from a culture that models self-criticism as a form of virtue and self-compassion as a form of indulgence.

The work of this chapter is not positive thinking. It is not replacing uncomfortable questions with cheerful ones and hoping the brain complies. It is something more precise: identifying the specific questions you ask yourself most often, testing them against a single criterion — are they designed to produce useful answers? — and replacing the ones that fail with questions that are honest and productive rather than honest and destructive.

* * *

Research on rumination and emotional regulation, developed particularly in the work of Ethan Kross at the University of Michigan, makes a distinction that is simple enough to seem obvious and important enough to change how you talk to yourself.

"Why" questions produce loops. "What" questions produce movement.

"Why am I so anxious about this?" has no useful answer, and the attempt to find one tends to deepen the anxiety rather than resolve it. The question invites an examination of root causes that the anxious person is poorly equipped to conduct — and the examination itself tends to generate more material for the anxiety to work with.

"What am I actually worried about?" is a different question entirely. It is specific, it is forward-looking, and it has a finite answer. And once you have that answer, the next question becomes: "What is one thing I could do about this today?" Not a solution. Just a next step. Just enough to shift the brain from surveillance mode — scanning for threat — into action mode, which is where it functions best.

The same principle applies across the full range of internal dialogue. "Why did I do that?" generates self-criticism and defends against nothing. "What was I trying to do, and is there a better way to get there?" generates learning and forward motion. "Why is this so hard?" confirms difficulty. "What would make this easier?" recruits the brain's problem-solving capacity rather than its self-punishing one.

* * *

The shift from backward to forward internal questioning is not about denying what went wrong. It is about directing the brain's attention toward the part of the situation it can actually do something about.

There is a practical complement to this reframe: the end-of-day question practice. This is among the most studied and most consistently effective small habits in the positive psychology and coaching literatures. Three questions, asked at the end of each day, for three to five minutes.

What went well today, and why? The "why" is essential. It moves the question from passive inventory to active learning — forcing the brain to identify the specific things you did or the conditions that produced a good outcome, which makes them more likely to be repeated.

What is one thing I would do differently tomorrow? Not a retrospective punishment, not a lengthy audit of failure. One thing. Specific. Actionable. The question that converts experience into improvement without requiring a performance review.

What am I looking forward to? This question is often underestimated. It ends the day oriented toward something rather than away from something — a small but meaningful shift in the brain's relationship with time.

Three questions. Five minutes at most. The compound effect of this practice over months and years is not dramatic insight. It is a different relationship with your own experience — more curious, more learning-oriented, more able to distinguish what you can change from what you cannot.

* * *

There is a harder question that deserves its own space, because it is the one most likely to change the big things.

"What would I tell a friend who was in exactly this situation?"

Most people hold themselves to a standard of self-examination that would strike them as cruel if it were applied to someone they love. They demand answers, assign blame, and refuse allowances that they would extend to a close friend without a second thought.

The question "what would I tell a friend?" activates a different mode of thinking — more generous, more problem-focused, more oriented toward what is actually useful. Research by Kristin Neff on self-compassion consistently shows that people who are able to offer themselves the same quality of care they would offer a friend make better decisions, recover from setbacks faster, and report higher wellbeing — not despite the self-compassion, but because of it.

This is not an argument for letting yourself off the hook. It is an argument for the kind of honest, warm, forward-oriented thinking that produces actual change — as opposed to the self-punishing kind, which mostly produces more of the same.

The Exercise

For the next seven days, end each day with three questions: What went well today and why? What is one thing I would do differently tomorrow? What am I looking forward to?

Write the answers down. The writing is not optional — it externalises the process, makes it observable, and makes it far more effective than simply thinking the questions.

At the end of seven days, notice whether your relationship with your own inner life feels different.

Chapter Summary

- The quality of your internal questions determines the quality of your thinking and your emotional experience. Most people run on questions designed to punish rather than to produce useful answers.

- "Why" questions tend to generate loops. "What" questions tend to generate movement. "Why am I anxious?" has no useful answer. "What am I worried about, and what is one thing I can do about it?" does.

- The shift from backward-looking to forward-looking internal questioning is not positive thinking. It is directing your brain's problem-solving capacity toward the part of the situation you can actually change.

- The end-of-day practice — what went well and why, what would I do differently, what am I looking forward to — produces a sustained reorientation toward learning and forward motion.

- "What would I tell a friend in this situation?" activates the honest, warm, forward-oriented thinking that produces genuine change, rather than the self-punishing kind that mostly produces more of the same.

Chapter 7

The Question Habit

There is a person in almost every organization — you may know one — who has a reputation for something they probably could not fully explain if asked.

They are known as someone worth talking to. When people leave a conversation with them, they feel clearer than before. Not because this person gave better advice than anyone else. Not because they are more knowledgeable or more experienced. Because somehow, in their presence, the person doing the talking does their best thinking. The problems get articulated more precisely. The solutions become more visible. The conversation itself does work that ordinary conversations do not.

What this person is almost certainly doing, whether consciously or not, is practising a small set of habits. Before significant conversations, they spend a few minutes thinking about what they actually want to understand. During conversations, they pause before they ask. Afterwards, they briefly reflect on what they learned and what they would do differently.

These are not personality traits. They are practices. And practices can be built.

* * *

Knowledge fades. Habits do not.

You have almost certainly read something before that changed how you thought — , clearly, with real conviction — and then found yourself, a month later, back in the same patterns, as if the reading had not happened. This is not a memory failure. It is the absence of a system. Understanding without structure produces intention without behavior. And the inside of most people's heads is already full of very good intentions that have not changed much.

The goal of this final chapter is not to add to that inventory. It is to give you a specific, minimal structure — three rituals, each taking no more than two minutes — that converts the understanding in this book into a different practice of conversation.

The three rituals are: the preparation practice, the in-conversation pause, and the review habit.

* * *

The preparation practice takes place before any conversation that matters to you — a difficult discussion with someone you care about, a significant meeting, a feedback conversation, an exchange with someone whose trust you are trying to earn.

Before the conversation, write down three things.

What do I actually want to understand from this conversation? Not what you want to say. Not the point you want to make. What you want to know. This single question redirects your preparation from performance to inquiry — from entering the conversation to impress to entering it to learn. It is, in practice, one of the most significant shifts available.

What am I assuming about this person or this situation that might not be true? This is the pre-conversation application of the audit from Chapter 1. It is the deliberate surfacing of the unconscious presumptions you are carrying — so that you can hold them loosely rather than having them run the conversation without your knowing.

What is the one question I most want to ask? Not a list. One. If you could learn only one thing from this conversation, what would it be? Having a single question as your anchor makes you less dependent on a prepared script — and more able to follow the conversation wherever it actually goes, because you know what you are ultimately there to find out.

Two minutes. Done in a notebook, on your phone, on the back of a receipt. What matters is that it is written, not just thought — because writing externalises the process and makes it real in a way that thinking about it does not.

The in-conversation pause is the practice described in the chapter on anatomy, brought forward here as a habit to build: the three-second gap between receiving an answer and asking your next question.

Most people use the time while someone else is speaking to compose their own next contribution. This is the primary mechanism that destroys conversational quality. It is not that such people are self-absorbed. It is that they have a brain that experiences conversational silence as a void that needs filling, and they fill it with preparation.

The in-conversation pause interrupts this. Before asking any question that matters, you take three seconds — , not performatively — and use that time not to compose but to receive. To let the previous answer arrive properly. To ask whether there is something in what was just said that is worth going deeper on before moving forward.

This is, in practice, also the space where follow-up questions are born. Spontaneous follow-ups — the ones that feel natural rather than formulaic — almost always emerge in the beat of genuine attention that precedes the next question. They are the product not of planning but of presence.

* * *

The review habit is the practice that closes the learning loop.

After any significant conversation — one that mattered, or one where something did not go the way you hoped — spend sixty seconds asking yourself three questions.

What did I learn that I did not know before? Not what happened in the conversation, but what new understanding you took from it. Making this explicit, even briefly, is what converts experience into development rather than just experience.

What question would have unlocked more? This is the habit of retrospective improvement — identifying the specific moment where a better question would have changed the direction, and noting what that question was. Over time, this builds a kind of conversational intelligence that cannot be taught directly: you start to recognize the type of moment that requires the type of question, because you have catalogued enough examples to notice the pattern.

What did I assume rather than ask? The habit of catching the moments when you presumed rather than inquired — and bringing that back into awareness — is what gradually closes the gap between the questions you ask and the ones you could ask.

Sixty seconds. The habit does not require more than that. What it requires is that you actually do it — not mentally, not occasionally, but after every conversation you care about. The cumulative effect of that practice, over months and years, is not easily overstated.

* * *

Habits work best when they are attached to existing cues. This is one of the most robust findings in the behavioural science of habit formation. New behavior is most reliably adopted when it is grafted onto an existing routine that already happens without effort — what the research calls "habit stacking."

The question is: which of the three rituals, attached to which existing habit, would change the most for you?

If you always take two minutes between your last meeting and the next one, that is the slot for the preparation practice. If you always walk from one place to another between conversations, that is the slot for the sixty-second review. If you always look at your phone before making a call, putting the phone down and writing one question instead is a habit stack that costs almost nothing and produces something real.

The point is not to find the perfect system. The point is to start with one practice, attached to one existing habit, that you can actually sustain — and let the others follow when the first one has become automatic.

* * *

Here is the honest truth about this skill: the benefits are not immediate and they are not dramatic. The first time you apply the preparation practice, the conversation will probably feel similar to conversations you have always had. The first time you use the reflect-back, the other person will probably not burst into tears of gratitude. The first few times you ask a better question instead of making a statement, nothing visible will change.

What changes slowly is the pattern. After a week of the end-of-day practice, the inner questions become a little more productive. After a month of follow-up questions in conversations that matter, people begin to feel something in your presence that they may not be able to name but will begin to seek out. After a year of consistently arriving at conversations with one question you most want answered, your decisions will be better and your relationships will be deeper — not dramatically, not all at once, but measurably.

The benefits compound. And compounding is invisible until it is not.

The Exercise

Choose one ritual. One only. The preparation practice, the in-conversation pause, or the review habit.

Decide which existing habit you will attach it to — the one you already never miss.

Start tomorrow.

Chapter Summary

- Knowledge fades. Habits do not. The goal is not more understanding. It is a specific, minimal structure that converts understanding into a different practice of conversation.

- The three rituals are: the preparation practice (two minutes before any important conversation), the in-conversation pause (three seconds before any question that matters), and the review habit (sixty seconds after any conversation worth learning from).

- Habits work best when attached to existing cues. Choose one ritual, identify the existing habit you will attach it to, and start with that.

- The benefits of this practice are not immediate or dramatic. They compound over time — and compounding is invisible until it is not.

- Start with one. Only one. Let the others follow.

Conclusion

A Better Question Changes Everything

Go back to the dinner table from the introduction.

The same scene: a Tuesday evening, the television on in the background, someone you love telling you about their week. But this time, somewhere in the middle of their second sentence, you do something different. You stop composing your response. You let what they are saying arrive. And when they finish, instead of answering, you ask.

Not "how was the rest of it?" Not "did that get resolved?" Something real. Something specific to the exact thing they just said. Something that tells them, in the asking of it, that you were here — fully, without reservation — for every word.

They pause. A real pause. And then they say something they were not planning to say. Something truer than the version they came with. Something that needed to be said, and would not have been, if you had done what you would ordinarily have done.

That is the scope of what this book is about. Not a dramatic transformation. Just a door, quietly opened — and what is on the other side of it.

* * *

You now have the tools. You understand why bad questions fail — the hidden jobs they are performing, the curse of expertise that stops the most knowledgeable people from asking, the silence that destroys questions before they can do their work. You know the structural qualities that make a great question great. You know the trust-building moves — the follow-up, the reflect-back, the permission question — and why they work when performed with presence. You have question sets for the meetings, the feedback conversations, the relationships, and the inner life. You have three rituals to make all of this a practice rather than a memory.

But the most important thing is not the specific questions in this book. It is the shift in orientation they represent.

A person who asks better questions is a person who has decided to be curious about the world — not just curious about their own conclusions. Who has decided that other people's experiences, perspectives, and inner lives are worth understanding — not just worth hearing long enough to respond to. Who has decided that the best conversations are not the ones where you said the most, but the ones where you learned the most.

That decision changes everything. The questions are just how you live it.

* * *

One thing this book has asked of you, quietly, in every chapter: the willingness to not know. To ask a question when a statement would feel safer. To wait in the silence when filling it would feel more comfortable. To follow what the other person says rather than where you had planned to go.

This is the courage the introduction named. And like all forms of courage, it does not arrive fully formed. It is built, slowly, through practice — through the small repeated choices to be curious instead of certain, present instead of prepared, interested instead of interesting.

You will have conversations that do not go the way you hoped. You will ask questions that land wrong, and miss the question that would have opened everything. This is not failure. It is the friction of a skill being developed. Every good questioner has had a hundred bad conversations on the way to becoming someone worth talking to.

What matters is the direction. And the direction is yours to choose.

Go ask something you do not know the answer to.

Appendix

The Quick-Reference Question Bank

QUESTIONS FOR WORK

- What problem are we actually trying to solve here?
- What are we assuming that might not be true?
- What would need to be true for this to fail?
- Imagine it is a year from now and this has failed. What went wrong?
- What does success look like from your perspective?
- What is the one thing we need to decide before we leave today?
- Who else is affected by this that is not in the room?
- What is one thing I could do differently that would make the biggest difference?
- How do you feel it went?
- Can you give me a specific example?
- What is the biggest obstacle you are running into right now?
- What would you do if you had twice the time? Half the resource?

QUESTIONS FOR RELATIONSHIPS

- What has been the best part of your week that I might not know about?
- What do you need from me right now — advice or just someone to listen?
- What is something you have been thinking about that you have not said yet?
- What is something you are excited about that you have not told many people?

- What do you wish I understood better about you?

- What have you changed your mind about recently?

- What do you wish people asked you more about?

- What has surprised you lately?

QUESTIONS FOR CHILDREN

- What was the hardest part of your day?

- What do you think would be fair in this situation?

- What are you proudest of that nobody noticed?

- What would you do differently if you were in charge?

- What are you looking forward to?

- What do you wish I asked you more about?

QUESTIONS TO ASK YOURSELF

- What am I assuming that might not be true?

- What is the most useful question I could be asking right now?

- What went well today, and why?

- What is one thing I would do differently tomorrow?

- What am I looking forward to?

- What would I tell a friend who was in exactly this situation?

- What was I trying to do, and is there a better way to get there?

- What would make this easier?

- What would I do if I knew I could not fail?

- What would I do even if I knew I might fail?

- What do I actually want here — and is what I am doing moving me toward it?

- What is one small thing I could do right now?

THE THREE-SECOND AUDIT (use before any question that matters)

1. Do I already know the answer I want?

If yes, make it a statement, not a question.

2. Am I asking this to fill silence or to hear the answer?

If it is to fill silence, wait three more seconds first.

3. Does this question embed an assumption about the right answer?

If yes, rewrite it with the assumption removed.

About the Author

Elias Grant writes practical, research-backed books on the specific micro-skills that most improve daily life. He focuses on the gap between knowing what would help and actually being able to do it — translating the best available research in psychology, neuroscience, and behavioral science into plain English and tools that work in ordinary, busy, imperfect lives. The Content 7 series is published by Asher Rohi Publishing.

Also by Asher Rohi Publishing

The Content 7 Series by Elias Grant

- Book 1 — Ask Better Questions: The One Skill That Improves Every Relationship and Meeting

- Book 2 — Sleep Like You Mean It: A No-Nonsense Guide to Better Rest

- Book 3 — Say No Without Guilt: How to Set Limits and Still Be Liked

- Book 4 — The 20-Minute Morning: A Simple System for Calm, Focused Days

- Book 5 — Read More, Remember More: How to Actually Finish Books and Use What You Learn

- Book 6 — Walk More, Live Better: How 30 Minutes a Day Changes Everything

- Book 7 — Digital Detox in 7 Days: Reclaim Your Focus Without Quitting the Internet

Visit asherrohipublishing.com for the latest releases.

Disclaimer

This book is intended for general informational and educational purposes only. It is not a substitute for professional medical, psychological, or other professional advice. Always seek qualified professional guidance before making significant changes to your health, sleep, diet, exercise habits, or professional practices. The author and publisher disclaim any liability arising directly or indirectly from the use or application of any information contained in this book.

A note from the publisher Asher Rohi Publishing is an independent press producing short, research-backed books on the micro-skills that most improve daily life. Every book in the catalogue is designed to be read in a few sittings and applied immediately.

If this book was useful, the most valuable thing you can do for it is leave an honest review at Amazon or the bookseller of your choice. Reviews are how independent books find new readers — even one or two sentences make a real difference.

To explore the rest of the series, sign up for new releases, or contact the publisher, visit asherrohipublishing.com.

Published by Asher Rohi Publishing asherrohipublishing.com First Edition, 2026 A catalogue record for this book is available from the National Library of Australia.

Published by Asher Rohi Publishing
asherrohipublishing.com
First Edition, 2026